SELLING
YOURSELF

THE JOURNEY TO
SALES SUCCESS

BRYAN FOSMORE

Jones Media Publishing
10645 N. Tatum Blvd. Ste. 200-166
Phoenix, AZ 85028
www.JonesMediaPublishing.com

Disclaimer:
The author strives to be as accurate and complete as possible in the creation of this book, notwithstanding the fact that the author does not warrant or represent at any time that the contents within are accurate due to the rapidly changing nature of the Internet.

While all attempts have been made to verify information provided in this publication, the Author and the Publisher assume no responsibility and are not liable for errors, omissions, or contrary interpretation of the subject matter herein. The Author and Publisher hereby disclaim any liability, loss or damage incurred as a result of the application and utilization, whether directly or indirectly, of any information, suggestion, advice, or procedure in this book. Any perceived slights of specific persons, peoples, or organizations are unintentional.

In practical advice books, like anything else in life, there are no guarantees of income made. Readers are cautioned to rely on their own judgment about their individual circumstances to act accordingly. Readers are responsible for their own actions, choices, and results. This book is not intended for use as a source of legal, business, accounting or financial advice. All readers are advised to seek the services of competent professionals in legal, business, accounting, and finance field.

Printed in the United States of America

ISBN: 978-1-948382-45-8 paperback

DEDICATION

I dedicate this book to all of my mentors. Thank you for believing in me, investing in me, and helping me to become a better version of myself. The high bar of excellence you set has pushed me to find my personal and professional best in everything I've done thus far.

I hope I made you proud and exceeded your expectations because that was always my goal in life. Now, my ongoing aspirational goal is to pay it forward and help others like you have helped me.

To my three mentors in heaven: Your life advice and career coaching were game-changing in my career development. I wish you were able to read this book to see the impact and influence you had on me.

ACKNOWLEDGEMENTS

I want to thank my fiancé, Jill, for her great advice and contributions to this book. We make a great team!

CONTENTS

FOREWORD

When Bryan knocked on my door twenty-five years ago, I immediately saw that he had a sincere passion and drive to succeed as well as a willingness to learn from others. He invited me to go fishing and it was the start to a long and wonderfully rewarding relationship. Bryan has always craved feedback, which is so important to learning and improving yourself. It has been a joy to mentor him over the course of his career and I am proud of his accomplishments. With all his success, he has stayed humble and mentored others, including my two sons. I have watched firsthand as Bryan has grown into a highly effective sales leader and his work ethic is second to none. He always wanted to be measured and his goal was to be the best at whatever he did.

I enjoyed reading "Selling Yourself: The Journey to Sales Success". I found it to be motivational and filled with practical advice that can help anyone in their career journey. This book has straightforward language and was written with the intention of helping the reader to grow. Everyone from a sales rep to a senior executive needs to have the ability to sell themselves in personal and professional settings in order to develop and lead others. You will find this book a very practical guide to success. I hope you will read and reference this handbook and put its wisdom to practice.

Lester B. Knight
Former Chairman and CEO, Allegiance Healthcare
Founding Partner, RoundTable Healthcare Partners
Chairman of the Board, Aon PLC

PREFACE

T hink BIG! One of my mentors challenged me to think big at a time when I had just been given the first great curveball of my career. My company had done a restructure that impacted my role as Senior Vice President of Sales. Suddenly, I was given the gift of time to reflect on what would be next. I had always wanted to write a book, and I felt this was my golden opportunity to take my shot at it.

Over my career, I have been blessed to work with so many talented leaders, co-workers, and customers, and I have felt compelled to give back in some way. This book presented a chance for me to pay it forward, sharing the knowledge and skills I've developed along the way. In addition, my nephew was just going into his junior year of college, majoring in business with the goal to have a career in medical device sales like me. I wanted to give him a great roadmap to help in his journey. There is nothing but a blue ocean on the horizon for him and absolutely no limits to what he can accomplish. And the same is true for you!

Working in sales is extremely challenging. Whether you are just starting your career, like my nephew, or you are 25 years into your career, this book is for you. The goal of this book is to help everyone become better at sales and to understand that sales is about selling YOURSELF.

With what I've learned, I want to help everyone accelerate their career in sales. There is an ocean of opportunity out there for you if you have the commitment to follow the roadmap. I feel confident you can become an *elite seller* if you put into practice all that my book will teach you.

Now, let's go and get after it! Many of my ideas might seem easy but – just remember – the challenge is having the discipline to put them into practice. It's time to start selling yourself!

CORPORATE REDNECK

**"Go knock on the CEO's door
and sell yourself."**

And thus began my career in medical device sales as my first business mentor encouraged me with these words. Have you ever found yourself looking for that first big breakthrough job in your career? A big promotion? Perhaps a career change to an entirely different industry?

This was my first big opportunity to sell myself with the goal of making an incredible first impression. It was my one shot to prove I should be considered for a job within the CEO's company. So, I knocked on the door, told the CEO I was interested in a sales job, and asked if he wanted to go fishing to get to know each other. He did, and a few weeks later I was flying to Chicago for an interview. My family members said, "Go sell yourself and win this job!" It felt like I had won the lottery, and there was no way I was going to waste this opportunity.

Have you ever felt like you wanted to get better at "selling yourself"? This book will help you improve at this– no matter who you are or what your profession is. My goal is to help you get better at "selling yourself" by providing practical experience and wisdom.

My story continued by asking for guidance from a guy who worked at the medical device company I was going to interview with. I asked him, "What do you recommend I do for the interview?" His advice was invaluable, and I remember him emphasizing to me at the very end of our talk to **"make sure you don't oversell yourself and don't undersell yourself."** This theme of "selling yourself" kept coming up early in my career and was ultimately my inspiration for writing this book.

I am originally from a small town in Northern Michigan, and my parents owned a small retail sporting goods store in this tourist town. The retail selling experience of dealing with the American public and doing guided fishing helped me to develop my selling skills. Hence the title of "Corporate Redneck." Now, I was going to have to sell myself for the biggest interview of my life and a job that could launch me into the medical device industry. Maybe I was clueless about a big corporate interview, but I wasn't clueless about how to connect with people because I had experienced great interactions with many people across all walks of life.

My experience in that retail store was invaluable to my career, inspiring me to strive for great success. We had customers from all classes of life. There were the under-resourced who never had money but certainly had time. There were the middle-class folks who worked hard and saved enough to be able to enjoy their hobbies on the weekends. Lastly, there were the rich who could buy whatever they wanted and do whatever they wanted. My goal was to become successful because I admired the wealthy people who had the money and freedom to do whatever they desired. It was at this point in my life that I realized I wanted to go from being a small town "redneck" to a successful businessperson.

It was so exciting pulling into the company's campus, complete with tall buildings, and busy professionals buzzing around. My preparation had me ready to win the job. The advice of not overselling myself was easy because it was so early in my career; my experience was limited. But I had to remember not to undersell myself either. I figured my desire, passion, and commitment would be unmatched by anyone with similar limited experience, and I made sure that I emphasized these traits during the interview. The job offer came about a week later, and this was the start of a career of selling myself.

I wrote this book to help you in your journey of "selling yourself." The truth is that you will be "selling yourself" throughout the course of your life. This book focuses on "selling yourself" professionally, but I am confident it can help many people improve selling themselves in *all* aspects of life.

The simple concepts in this book will help you to grow and develop in your sales career. Simple doesn't always translate to easy, so it is important that you follow a process. While my background is in medical device sales, this book can help anyone– from college students to tenured sales professionals.

The book is broken into seven main chapters, each one building from the last. Each chapter has three main subtopics to simplify and consolidate each lesson. I know from experience that sales reps love things that are easy to read. This book will be a journey of stages of "selling yourself" that will help guide you, and each chapter will end with key summary points.

The stages of this book are as follows:

- **Pre-Forming—"Grow Roots Before the Fruits"**
- **Forming—"Own Your Career"**

- **Pre-Storming—"Plan Your Work, and Work Your Plan"**
- **Storming—"Show Up"**
- **Pre-Performing—"Prepare to Win"**
- **Performing—"Win the Day"**
- **Overachieving—"Rise to the Next Level"**

CHAPTER 1

PRE-FORMING – "GROW ROOTS BEFORE THE FRUITS"

Pre-Forming is all about starting with the right foundation. Your goal is to get off to a great start whether you are starting a new job, promoting up, or changing careers entirely. I was so excited to begin my sales career for a medical device company called *Allegiance Healthcare*. I was pumped to start putting into practice all the great knowledge I had gained in training and to start selling products. Everything was lining up for me to be successful, and I had the right personal characteristics to win. It was during my first meeting with the Chief Operating Officer – who would later become one of my favorite mentors over my career – where I heard the best advice.

"Bryan, it is not about selling widgets. It is about selling *yourself.*"

Those words were so powerful, and I have never forgotten them in over 25 years in sales. It also interested me that this was the third successful businessperson who had inferred sales was really about "selling yourself." It became a calling and a theme to my sales career; I became committed to the key personal characteristics that would help me to *sell myself.*

The key elements for success I want to share with you are what I call "The Foundational Four." These four characteristics are especially important in building the right foundation during the Pre-Forming stage that is all about you as an individual. My sales representative peers who were successful embodied these characteristics over 25 years ago, and these same traits will help you to differentiate yourself in today's world.

PART I: IT STARTS WITH YOU

The Foundational Four

1. Personal Drive

Personal drive is *essential* to finding success in sales. It is critical that you have the inner drive to win. I like this saying: **"Motivation comes from within, and consequences come from *without.*"** It really starts with having the drive to be successful because you will need to be in control of your own career. You will see people who are blessed with talent but lack the *personal drive* to maximize it to get everything they can out of their God-given gifts.

Why does personal drive matter? Nobody will own your career like you will. You should passionately chase your dreams. Personal drive is all about making the most impact in every role and giving your best self. Personal drive means having the inner mindset to go the extra mile at every point in your career.

2. Winning Attitude

Having a winning attitude is so important. In our professional and personal lives, we all face challenges that are both in and out of our control. The key is how we *respond* to those challenges. **A person with a winning attitude will always focus on what they can control rather than what they cannot control.** They bring a growth mindset to work that is contagious to everyone they work with.

Why does a winning attitude matter? A winning attitude will help you to always stay focused on the positive. As you move along in your career, you'll find there are those who make excuse after excuse as to why they can't find success, letting every obstacle impact their attitude– for the worse. The key is to always keep a winning attitude. This will set you apart from others. Companies, bosses, and co-workers love people who bring a winning attitude to the workplace because it encourages, motivates, and lifts everyone else to do better and to be better.

3. People Skills

People skills enable you to work well with others. In your career, you will be working with all types of different personalities. It is important you find a way to connect with all the people you will be dealing with, both internally and externally. The best employees I've worked with have found ways to relate effectively and have good relationships with everyone. It is important to know a person's personality type in advance because then you can find the best ways to connect with them.

Why does having people skills matter? People skills help you to build quality relationships– and sales is all about relationships. Additionally, having great people skills will help to accelerate your career because you work well with others internally and externally.

4. Results-Driven

Being results-driven means you are always focused on creating winning results. Companies will stretch you to hit goals, providing incentives for reaching and overachieving goals. You want to make sure you are results-focused because, in every job, it is all about your performance and the contributions you make to the company. Just showing up and trying to survive in a job is aiming too low and, in most cases, will lead to a short and unproductive sales career.

Why does being results-driven matter? Results determine your pay and your advancement in your career. You will be successful and get promoted when you drive results that help grow a company and improve their bottom line. Sales is all about performance and driving growth, so being results-driven is a key characteristic that leads to a lifetime of success.

Embodying The Foundational Four should really position you well to sell yourself. I will be sharing other key success factors that will help you, but it is critical that you have the right personal characteristics. The next part in Pre-Forming is finding mentors to help you to grow.

PART II: YOUR MENTORS

The mentor who told me to knock on the CEO's door ended up becoming the best mentor I could have asked for in the Pre-Forming stage. We developed a relationship while I was working at my parents' retail sporting goods shop. This mentor was so kind, generous, humble, and successful. I wanted to be like him because he did everything first class and the right way.

After getting to know me, he said, "Bryan, you need to get out of this small town and aim big in your career. You could be a CEO someday because you have the right skills."

That was so empowering to me, and it gave me so much confidence that someone so successful would give me that type of encouragement and endorsement. We all need someone to inspire us and coach us to look beyond our limited scope of life. I grew up in a small town and now I had someone pushing me to shoot for the stars and start my career in a big city like Chicago.

My advice is to seek out mentors. Successful people like to pay it forward to others. Find someone you admire, and be fearless and just ask them to share about their experiences. You may be surprised how willing people are to give you advice and encouragement. My goal was to have multiple mentors because you can learn so much from everyone. It is great to get different perspectives from different people at all levels of an organization and of various tenures and job functions.

Below are some examples of my mentors. These types of people are ones you could seek out in the Pre-Forming stage. It is very important to have a variety of mentors who all bring something different to help you.

Mentor # 1: A Person I Admire Professionally

My first professional mentor was the guy who told me to go knock on the CEO's door. He was a successful partner at a very successful investment banking firm. He provided great encouragement and advice.

Mentor # 2: Sales Professional Peer

The rep I talked to who helped me with my first big job interview always gave great advice and encouragement. He has been a lifelong friend and mentor, personally and professionally.

Mentor # 3: Human Resource Executive

This executive was a tremendous help to me in the *Forming* stage of my career. I will talk about him in the next chapter. He was one of the finest men I have ever met.

Mentor # 4: My First Mentor in a Field Sales Job

This rep was one of the top reps in the country who won "Rookie of the Year" and later "Rep of the Year". She taught me the importance of customer relationships and how to be a field sales representative.

Mentor # 5: CEO

The CEO whose door I knocked on ended up becoming a great mentor to me. It does not get any better than knowing the person at the top of the food chain. He was, and still is, a great friend and mentor. He has been extremely successful and sets a high standard of excellence in everything he does.

You will accelerate the Pre-Forming process by finding great mentors who will help you to grow faster and better professionally. Now, I'll explain the importance of networking to help you to expand your reach.

PART III: NETWORKING

Networking is important over the course of your entire career but it's especially important in the early years. To me, networking is building an extension of your mentors and the next logical step in expanding the coalition of people who can help you in your career. Your mentors can connect you to their close friends and work connections. Below, I break networking opportunities down into four key groups.

Mentors' Friends

You will see that the friends of your mentors will always want to help their friends. If your mentor is willing to endorse you to one of their friends, then you know you have a great relationship. You should aim to get connected to five of your mentors' key contacts.

Mentors' Work Connections

Your mentors' work connections are very helpful before and after you get a job. It might be a human resources connection who helps you with interviewing or a sales leader who gives you advice on selling. The key is to make a great first impression and listen to their advice. Your mentors' work connections might even help you land an interview where you will have to sell yourself to win the opportunity.

Your Friends' Connections

Your friends or family friends know you intimately, so they have a really good idea of how you would be early in your career on the job. They can introduce you to their connections who may be able to help you. Sometimes it just takes one person who is willing to endorse you with a letter of recommendation or a phone call.

Your Work Connections

As you dive into your career, you'll develop work connections and expand your relationships. This is the best networking option in my opinion because you get a chance to really see who you connect with the best and who can help accelerate your career. I loved connecting with people who inspired me and influenced me to want to get better and be better. You can learn so much from your work connections and their career paths.

Summary:

- **It Starts with YOU:** Embody The Foundational Four and focus on "selling yourself" rather than widgets.

- **Your Mentors:** Find mentors and look to them for career advice.

- **Networking:** Build and expand your professional network.

CHAPTER 2

FORMING – "OWN YOUR CAREER"

"You have to own your career!"

T his was advice given to me by my mentor who was a senior Human Resources executive. My first job in healthcare was the lowest level sales job in inside sales. For me, the goal was to learn the business from the ground up and, most importantly, to be around all the talent and experience at the corporate office. This was absolutely the best option for me in the Forming stage of my career. In a very short period of time, I was playing basketball with some executives in a league, and simultaneously growing my network. I realized this experience at the corporate office was going to fast track my career and quickly learned it was my personal responsibility to develop my career strategy and accept feedback and coaching, putting everything I learned into practice.

PART I: CAREER STRATEGY

My mentor who was in Human Resources sat down with me, and we started to map out a career strategy plan. The goal was to define where I wanted to be by 25 years old, 30 years old, 35 years old, and 40 years old.

These were the career milestones I set for myself:

- 25 - Specialty Field Sales Representative
- 30 - Regional Sales Manager
- 35 - Vice President of Sales
- 40 - Senior Vice President of Sales

You should set your own career milestones and then map out the skills necessary to achieve these goals. Your mentors can help you to determine the key skills needed to advance your career (e.g. communication skills, organizational skills, strategic planning skills, etc.). Even if you have a good baseline of skills, you still need to be willing to adapt, change, and grow your skillset to get to the next level for each promotion. In addition to having a career strategy, you need to be willing to accept feedback and coaching to fast-track your career development.

PART II: FEEDBACK + COACHING = DEVELOPMENT

Feedback

Many people refer to feedback as the **"breakfast of champions"** because feedback is so critical to our personal and professional growth. I was very eager to receive feedback early in my career because the more that people pointed out ways for me to improve, the faster I could grow into a bigger role. Feedback is important to receive but it's also important to *give...* to your manager, peers, and even friends.

Most of us have "blind spots," so it is important that someone points out to us if we are doing something wrong or could do it better. We also need positive feedback that reinforces our behaviors when we are on the right track and doing things the right way. All feedback is valuable and can help us to improve.

Coaching

Coaching is very important in your personal and professional development. It is especially important early in your career because coaching is what makes you better. A coach really invests in you by providing you with valuable insights into how you can improve. A coach is often a manager and typically has more experience than you, and that great expertise will help you.

I would not be where I am today without great coaching from the managers in my career. Coaching is so important because you can improve your results when someone helps you figure out how to achieve better results in the right way. My first managers really had to help me funnel my energy and passion into crisp and clear sales messaging. I knew I had the right personality to be successful, but I had to learn how to present to my customers in a more effective way.

The key is for you to *accept* the coaching. My high school basketball coach taught us to say "Thanks, Coach" every time he coached us. It trains the heart and mind to accept the coaching and be appreciative that your coach is investing in you. As an employee, you should be thankful when people are working to help you get better.

Development

The combination of feedback and coaching will lead to your *development*. One of my former CEO's used to say, **"We all need to be lifelong learners."** I think that to be a lifelong learner you must be able to accept feedback and coaching along the way so you can learn and grow in your personal and professional development. You should want to be developed into a better human in all aspects of life; but you need to be proactive and ask for feedback and coaching, especially if you're not getting the results you desire.

Early in your career, you will begin to identify the strengths you have that will help set you apart from your peers. You want to be cautious that you don't overuse a strength because it could hurt you later in your career if you become too one-dimensional, relying on one of your go-to strengths. An example would be someone with great interpersonal skills who might become too reliant on getting by on their personality alone versus being well-rounded with financial discipline, operational expertise, business acumen, etc.

PART III: KNOWING SKILLS TO DOING SKILLS

Feedback, coaching, and development is worthless if you don't do anything with it. The Forming stage is all about taking ownership and personal accountability to get better. Don't fall victim to hearing feedback and thinking to yourself that it is very basic and easy. Just because things are easy doesn't mean people necessarily do them.

Doing skills is when you actually put the feedback you've received into practice. You can't just be a talker in sales– you need to put your money where your mouth is and be a doer too! **If you want to**

get good at "selling yourself," then you need to get good at taking feedback and putting it into practice.

Your managers and mentors will continue to invest in you with great advice throughout your career if they see that you actually work to get better. We should all feel blessed to have someone care enough about us to coach us because it takes discipline and effort to provide such insight. The best coaches will make you better and will give you the right coaching at the right time. You just need to have the discipline to apply the coaching to your daily job.

It is really a personal choice to want to improve your skills. There is a saying that **"dull knives don't cut, and rusty keys don't open locks."** It is *so* important to invest in yourself and your career for your personal development. It really all boils down to having the relentless drive to improve ourselves. If you are lucky enough to get good training, then it is critical to put that training into practice, taking it from the *knowing* skills to the *doing* skills. So much training is lost over time if it is not put into practice to make it a habit.

Doing skills is all about just getting started by **beginning** to do something. This is sometimes the hardest step in the process—to just get moving. In my experiences, both with myself and with peers, I've found that **good things happen when you have a bias for action to just go and get in front of customers.**

Most likely, once you begin actively calling on customers, you will start **"questioning"** some things. *Could I have done this better? Should I have done this differently? How can I repeat those behaviors to get the same results?* The experience of *doing* shows us some things that went well and some things that didn't go well. Getting out and making things happen that lead to the questioning phase is so much better than not even beginning to get out of the blocks to do something.

Lastly, you hope you will be **transformed** by doing things that will create muscle memory, great habits, and behaviors. We all become such creatures of habit, so you really want to start building great practices early in your career. I always believed it was important to get in front of customers and enjoyed that more than working from my home office. Push yourself to the doing skills because it is never enough to just have the knowing skills. There are a lot of smart people out there who don't take the initiative to make things happen. The risk of doing nothing is a pretty big risk. Instead, take the risk to get out of your comfort zone and get out there.

Summary:

- **Career Strategy:** Build a career strategy.

- **Feedback + Coaching = Development:** Embrace working to get better.

- **Knowing Skills to Doing Skills:** Put into practice what you have learned.

CHAPTER 3

PRE-STORMING – "PLAN YOUR WORK, AND WORK YOUR PLAN"

Pre-Storming is all about planning and preparation. I remember a story from my days of being a specialty rep that demonstrates the importance of planning. We had a two-week training class and, on the final day, we were going to do a role play in front of the group. I was so pumped up to talk about everything I had learned in the class over the last two weeks. Our training manager was a former Operating Room Director. She played the role of a tough, busy customer with a get-to-the-point type of personality which is very common with Operating Room Managers. Her goal was to make this activity both realistic and stressful.

I came into the role play extremely excited to tell the customer how great our products were and how wonderful our company was. My goal was to really hit all the selling points and convince the customer that we were the best choice for her. Unfortunately, I failed to prepare to make sure I was asking the *right* questions. The result was too much selling and telling to the customer and not enough asking and *listening to the needs of the customer*.

The feedback I received was that I came into the call too aggressively by talking too much and not asking any probing questions. It was important feedback and a great moment in my development process. The training manager said she loved my passion and energy but that I did not ask any discovery questions to understand what the customer was really looking for. The role play provided me with humbling feedback, but I appreciated the coaching because the training manager was just trying to make me more effective in my selling style. That experience emphasized to me the importance of planning.

Looking at your new sales role at a macro level and planning your sales strategy is what I refer to as Pre-Storming. It includes conducting an initial business assessment, developing your 30-60-90 day goals, and planning territory and time management.

PART I: BUSINESS ASSESSMENT

The Who?

You will want to build your knowledge of *who* the current customers are and how the sales are trending with those customers. It is best to start with your top 10 accounts because you always want to make sure you know your best customers first and the reasons why they buy. In many companies, you will find **there is an 80/20 rule; 80% of the business will be coming in from 20% of the customers.** You want to start by understanding how strong the customer relationships have been with the former rep and your company. You want to determine who the key decision makers are so you can start building relationships with them. The key is knowing the right people because so much of selling is making sure that you are selling to the main stakeholders who make the buying decisions.

The What?

You will want to start to focus on the products you will be selling and how to position those products to sell them most effectively. In many sales jobs, you may be selling multiple products. It is important to stay focused on the key products, or you'll risk becoming overwhelmed trying to sell too much. Additionally, your customer does not want to be sold a whole bunch of products at once. My advice is always to start with just selling one product in your bag. In reality, **the first few sales calls will really be about "selling yourself" by starting to establish some credibility with your customers.**

The Why?

The why is very important because customers buy for their own reasons and not necessarily the reasons that we want to sell to them. You should focus on what your customer wants, putting their needs above everything else. "Selling yourself" is way more important than selling a widget because your reputation is going to be what is most important in the short- and long-term. Customers are looking for reps and companies that can help them with their pain points or provide products or services that will bring them great value. This is where you hear the saying, **"Customers don't care how much you know as much as they care about how much you care."**

The Where?

The size of your territory and the location of your current and future customers are very important. This information helps you to think about your call pattern and where you will spend your time. For example, if all of your top 10 customers are spread out across a big geography, it would make it very difficult to service them at the level you would be aiming for. Your best customers expect to see a rep on a frequent basis; they require and need help from a sales rep. Unfortunately, if you are not present in the account, you will have a declining relationship with your customer and risk losing business.

The When?

You will find out in sales that *time* is one of the most critical factors. There are only so many hours in the day and days in the week that you can be selling to your customers. It is critical that you figure out the best time to call on customers to have the most impact. This includes knowing the best day of the week as well as the best time of day to meet with each customer.

The above questions are important to understand so that you can start to build your plan of attack. The biggest mistake you can make as a new rep is to visit customers without a good plan; you must get to know the background of your customers and prepare to make the most of those initial sales calls.

PART II: 30-60-90 DAY GOALS

The 30-60-90 plan sets the right objectives for the first few months of a new sales role. In some cases, you will be asked to provide this during a final interview for a job because the hiring company wants to understand your strategic thinking ability. The key to "selling yourself" is making sure you have a great plan, regardless of what the company has prepared for your first 90 days.

Sales is all about momentum, and it is important to get a fast start in your new role to make a great first impression. You won't get a second chance at starting relationships with your customers, so this is an important step in "selling yourself." We will now look at some of the things you can do in sales regardless of whether you are a new rep or a tenured rep going into a new job. In the first 30 days, there will be a great deal of learning and reacting to customer requests as you ramp up knowledge of your company and products.

First 30 Days

The first 30 days will typically consist of some type of orientation training. This will be conducted at home or at a corporate office, providing you with basic knowledge about the company and products. Your manager will help to guide you in focusing on key priorities during the on-boarding process. You will want to start getting a basic understanding of your territory from a sales trending perspective to see how the business has performed before. You will assess your territory in terms of the *Who, What, Why, Where, and When.*

Initially, you will want to get connected to your top 10 customers. The objective is to just "be known" by your top customers so they have a point of contact. Right away, your focus should simply be to introduce yourself to your best accounts. You want to ask some great discovery questions and make sure your highest priority is checking to see if they have any immediate needs or wants you can assist with. The first 30 days is just about making a great first impression with your top accounts and helping them.

30 to 60 Days

Hopefully, you will have had the chance to meet with your top 10 accounts in the first 30 days to establish yourself as their new sales representative. If you couldn't meet with them face-to-face due to training or scheduling conflicts, you will want to get this accomplished in the 30 to 60 day timeframe. You will also be responding to follow-up requests from those initial meetings along with any new customer requests you get from those outside of your top 10. You will start to put your training knowledge to work by promoting certain products from your orientation product training during follow-up meetings with your top 10 customers. With each sales call, you will continue to gather customer information by asking basic customer profiling questions.

60 to 90 Days

Sixty days into your plan, and after multiple customer visits, your mission is for customers to like you enough to start buying from you. You'll become liked by asking great questions, following up, bringing in great products, and providing many other sources of value. The goal is for the customer to start giving you some basic requests for information like cross-referencing and quoting so you can demonstrate your ability to follow up and follow through for their needs and wants. The repetitive sales call visits to the same customers will establish credibility and, hopefully, you will have had some good opportunities to delight the customer. You will earn their trust by being very responsive to their requests and showing up routinely to help them with good support and service for your product lines.

The 30-60-90 goals are all about "selling yourself." You want to be known because you will never sell anything if a customer doesn't know how to get a hold of you or your company. Then, you need to do everything you can to differentiate yourself and stand out in a positive way so customers will like you enough to give you new sales opportunities. Lastly, you earn their trust with the ultimate goal of having them call you *first*. The initial 90 days in a new sales role is so important in "selling yourself" and it is critical that you are highly efficient in your territory and time management.

PART III: TERRITORY AND TIME MANAGEMENT

The next key to Pre-Storming is territory and time management. You need to make great decisions on where to best spend your time. You will start to segment your customers by where you want to target your selling efforts.

Segmentation

The segmentation process will help you build your sales strategy in your 30-60-90 day goals to start really drilling down into your action plan. I like to separate the accounts into A accounts, B accounts, and C accounts.

The A accounts will be your *best* accounts. These accounts will do the most sales volume with you and are where you should have the best relationships. You want to make sure that you are visiting your A accounts on a weekly or bi-weekly basis, if possible, because competitors are always after your business. It is critical that you are there because even your best accounts can forget about you or fail to prioritize you if they don't see you; out of sight, out of mind as they say! Stay visible and active in these accounts and *always* bring and document value.

The B accounts are good accounts that just might be slightly below the top A accounts in sales volume. The major difference is that you don't have as much of the business as in your top accounts, and you typically will not have as many relationships. You also might not have as strong of relationships (because your competitor has them) since this isn't an account where you have the majority of the market share. Your focus is always working to move your B accounts to A accounts because you already have a great base of established business with them. It is much easier to grow an existing account where you have some relationships and some base business. You will want to try and see your B accounts bi-weekly or monthly, depending on the size of your territory and the number of accounts you call on.

The C accounts are the accounts with the *most* potential. These accounts are where you do very little business today and have very few relationships. You want to always be checking in with your C accounts but not at the frequency that you visit the A and B accounts. It is great to hit these accounts if they are geographically close to better accounts because it doesn't take a lot of effort to stop in if you happen to be in the area. For C accounts, you will want to try and see them monthly or quarterly, depending on the geographic location and how convenient it will be to stop in to visit them. These accounts will always have a lot of potential but will always be the hardest to grow because there are probably some strong reasons why they are not an A or B account. Your focus will be on probing to find out what they love about your competitors and figuring out some things they dislike about your competitors to determine how you can earn more new business.

Targeting

Once you have segmented your customers, you can start looking at *targeting*. It is important to target your top accounts first to make sure that you protect your base business and work hard to get your best customers to buy more from you. The sales numbers will tell you how much sales volume you have in those accounts and then you can start targeting product lines where you know you don't have all the business. It is nice when you have some business because it gives you a launching pad to sell from. Then, you can look at gaps where you can pull through other complimentary products you don't currently sell to that customer. Current customers can introduce you to other customer contacts within those top accounts. Then, your goal is to get your customers to refer you to another account if they would be willing to recommend you.

Time Management

Time is the most valuable asset you have in sales. You do not want to waste your time or your customers' time. I have heard that there are only 192 actual selling days a year– once you back out weekends, paid holidays, sick days, vacation days, meetings, training days, and administrative office days. The key is to be smart with your time management and make each day count.

Discipline is critical to effective time management because you will always have competing priorities that can be distractions. My fiancé likes the concept of **"Return on Time"** – the idea that you should spend your time working on the opportunities that will yield the most sales dollars. Therefore, pre-call planning becomes so important so you can thoughtfully think through how to best spend your precious time.

Summary:

- **Business Assessment:** Have a sales plan and work it.
- **30-60-90 Day Goals:** Be crystal clear in your goals for the first 90 days.
- **Territory and Time Management:** Be efficient and effective with your time.

CHAPTER 4

STORMING – "SHOW UP"

Some of the best advice I ever received came from a training class when I was starting out in sales. We were questioned about what we thought were the most important factors to being a good sales rep. The answers were across the board, from needing to be aggressive or personable, to being a hard worker or a great listener. Then, one of the reps said, **"You need to show up!"** She followed that with a statement that I always use now as a sales leader: **"The two hardest doors to open are the door to your house and the door to your car."**

Good things will happen when you get out in front of existing and potential customers. No sales are ever made by doing nothing or not taking a shot at trying to get a sale. Showing up seems very easy, but it takes a great deal of discipline and personal motivation to do it on a consistent basis.

I shared the planning and preparation required to understand your territory at a macro level in the Pre-Storming chapter. Now, it is time to start "Storming" by making sales calls. Don't sit back waiting for emails to come in and think that is sales. You need to take the initiative to get out and see customers face-to-face. Get up and get moving!

PART I: PREPARING FOR THE SALES CALL

We just learned the importance of "showing up" and now we will focus on key actions for when you leave the house. We will get to the disciplined selling process and the actual sales call after I outline the basics you need to consider.

Pre-Call Sales Planning

You want to have a great day of sales calls prepared in advance of leaving your home. The number of sales calls you will make each day is dependent on the anticipated length of each sales call and the distance between them. You want to have set appointments so that you can be laser-focused on your purpose for each sales call. For every sales call, you want to have your single sales objective established in advance so you can be proactively working to get new business or following up from a previous sales call. You want to be prepared for any questions your customers might ask. Additionally, you should know the questions you want to ask the customer based on where the conversation goes in the sales calls. Pre-call sales planning will help you sell more and sell *better* because you can't afford to just show up making sales calls without a plan. Showing up is important, but it will be much more effective when you are ready in advance of the sales call. You will make the biggest impact and have the most influence helping your customer improve their current condition when you are prepared.

Dress for Success

It is important to dress appropriately for your audience. I recommend having a professional business look. The world is becoming more casually dressed, but you want to make a great first impression. It is always better to be overdressed than underdressed. Let the customer give you permission to dress less formally over time. In healthcare, many reps will wear scrubs because they are working directly with end user nurses and doctors, so that is acceptable. The same is true for those who are actively servicing an account. I wouldn't recommend wearing scrubs or casual clothing to meet with someone for the first time. **Bring your best self!**

Bring a Computer or iPad

You should always be prepared for the sales call with supportive technology. I recommend having your computer or iPad so you can show presentations to your customers electronically or have access to other information. You can handle some customer requests in real time and make a great impression by doing so.

You will also be able to complete work in between sales calls. You can focus on making updates to your CRM tool, like Salesforce. This electronic tool will hold your key sales information. You want to maximize the hours of the workday so you don't have to cut into your evenings and weekends. By having your computer with you, you can make your updates in real time.

Carry Business Cards/Literature

Make sure you travel with business cards on every sales call because your goal is to meet new customer contacts every day. Providing a new customer with your business card will allow them to easily reach you. It is also important to have hard copies of literature with you because some customers will prefer that instead of electronic versions. The key is having the right product information at the right time so you can have the most effective sales call.

Take Samples

Samples are important in sales because customers love to touch and feel products. You can't just rely on selling off your computer. Samples help the sales call because you can hand the customer the product and let them give you some feedback with their initial reactions. Sometimes they might give positive feedback and selling points based on their experience that you didn't even consider. You might also get some negative feedback or ideas of ways to potentially make the product better which can also be very helpful.

Organize Your Car

Your car is your mobile office, so you want to make sure you have everything organized in your trunk. You should have literature, samples, and any other key company information. Your car should have your phone charger, a cooler for drinks and food, and anything you will need for that day to be successful. You should keep your car clean and organized. You want to display your professional best when your manager or anyone from your company does a ride-along with you. The key is always having everything you need for that day in your car.

Your sales calls will go much more smoothly when you are prepared. In addition to taking the actions I just shared, you must follow a disciplined sales process so you can create new opportunities and advance existing sales opportunities. This disciplined sales process will set you up to maximize your time and selling efforts.

PART II: DISCIPLINED SELLING PROCESS

A disciplined sales process will enable you to build a sales pipeline with sales opportunities in various stages. The sales process can be broken down into three main steps for the purposes of simplification. First, you need to create demand for a sale. This is generally called the *qualification* or *targeting* stage. The next step is showing the product, which often involves in-servicing or evaluation. Lastly, once you get commitment from the customer, you will be focused on the service and support stage. Before diving into these three stages in more detail, let's look at the importance of customer relationships in the disciplined selling process.

Relationships

Relationships are critical to the sales process. **People buy from people they like!** Your goal is to always build quality relationships with your customers. Putting the customer first is important because selling is always about prioritizing your customers' needs over your own personal needs and wants. As you build relationships, you will want to find champions, influencers, and supporters.

Champion

A customer champion is someone who will help you and coach you in the sales process. The bigger a sale is or the more complex the sales cycle, the more important the champion is. This person can help you to figure out how to navigate through the account to achieve your sales goal. A champion is a person who gives you a lot of valuable insight. This person can provide great information about the people you are trying to connect with who will be important in your selling process.

Influencers and Supporters

Another key group of customer contacts fall into the category of influencers and supporters. These customers can help you with your sales efforts. In more complex sales opportunities, you will need people who will help to influence the key decision maker. Influencers tend to be the type of personalities who will speak up and have a lot of input in the decision-making process. You will also want to have supporters who might not be as vocal as the influencers, but who can also be very helpful. The worst-case scenario is having people working against you who don't want to see you succeed or have an ulterior motive, like a relationship with another vendor who they are trying to protect. It is very important to make sure you build as many relationships as you can so that you have great depth and breadth in your customer contacts.

Sales Process

Now, we will transition into the sales process and keep it very simple. We are going to look at it in three steps: creating demand, showing the product, and servicing and supporting the product once the customer has purchased it.

Sales Process: Target Stage (Create Demand)

The first part of the sales process is the target stage with the goal to create demand for the product you are selling. Targeting is all about qualifying your opportunity. You want to ask some good discovery and clarifying questions to gauge the probability of you winning the opportunity. If you get some good buying signs from the customer (e.g. they would like to see the product, get the price of the product, or evaluate the product), then the opportunity can move to the next stage.

Sales Process: Active Stage (In-Service/ Conduct Evaluation)

The next step in the sales process is typically some form of show-and-tell. The request for a sample and pricing is a great step forward in the sales process. Next, in the same active stage, the customer might ask you to provide a demonstration or in-service of the product to show how it works. Then, in some cases, a customer might ask you if they can evaluate or trial the product to make sure it does everything you have told them it will do for them.

The champion will continue to help coach you in every stage of the sales process. In this active stage, they can help you identify who needs to see the samples, who needs to be in-serviced on the product, and also who could possibly want to evaluate the product. You will want to make sure that you have a good process to document the feedback from the customer. Most companies will have a set process for how to best provide an in-service and an evaluation backed up by documents that can help capture the feedback.

The goal is for the in-service and evaluation to go very smoothly with positive feedback from all the key decision makers. If everything goes well, they will be asking you for a final price quote so they can make a decision. Your goal is to get commitment with a purchase order. Once you get the customer commitment and they place an order, you can then transition to the final step of service and support.

Sales Process: Commit Stage (Service/Support)

The commit stage is the last step in a basic sales process. This stage is all about wonderful service and support. It is great to win new business, but it is equally important to *keep* the business. Support is critical because you always want to help your customer with any questions. Service is an on-going process that needs to be exceptional. **Great service is the best thing you can provide to keep the business you have.** Every customer loves great service and working with a rep and company that they can trust and always count on to deliver.

Service is *everything* in sales. This is so important in "selling yourself" because you want your personal brand to be putting the customer first in everything you do. Great service will separate you from your competition. Service is all about hard work and showing up more than other vendors. This shows your customer how committed you are.

PART III: THE SALES CALL

The actual sales call should be the easiest part of *Storming*. You should be ready because you have done all the sales call prep. Your disciplined sales process will keep you laser-focused and set on what needs to be done. I was taught in training to make sure to **have a single sales objective for each sales call so that you come in with a clear mission of what you want to accomplish.** Your sales call should be planned out around what needs to be done based on the stage that your opportunity is in. The key is when you first show up to start every meeting with a "thank you."

Say "Thank You!"

"Thank you" is a very powerful gratitude to share with your customer. In my experience, starting every meeting with a genuine "thank you" helps everything go much better. Thank your customer for their time, their current business, and their willingness to hear what you have to offer. I find that a lot of reps do not always display the gratitude they should towards customers. They can hire or fire any of us by where they spend their money. It is so easy to express gratitude and it goes a long way.

Plus, your customer will typically be much more relaxed after you thank them. They quickly start to see that you really appreciate their business and that you show humility; you don't want to be a sales rep who is all about your own success and personal commissions because customers will read right through that. Thanking your customer is important regardless of how much or how little business you have. After this step, you can start to transition into your sales messaging.

Deliver Your Sales Messaging

You want to make sure your sales messaging to the customer is crisp and clear. The goal for sales messaging is to make your points in as few words as possible. The sales messaging needs to be relevant and meaningful to the customer so they can see how your product can meet their specific needs. We always want to sell the customer on why our product will help them with driving results, benefits, advantages, and outcomes. We will go deeper into sales messaging in a later chapter and how to continuously improve your sales messaging using sales tools.

Ask Probing Questions and Listen to Your Customer

Listening is *critical* in sales. You should focus on asking the probing questions that you prepared in advance of your sales call. Customers really appreciate great questions that help them think critically about issues. The goal is to help the customer improve their current condition with your product. You can ask discovery questions, clarifying questions, and impact questions to help your customer think differently about what you are offering them. The key is to then *listen* to what they say. You may find that their needs or concerns lead you to offering a different product or solution.

Take Notes

Taking notes is very important in the sales call. Active listening requires writing down the information you are gaining from the customer. I have personally watched reps who don't take notes; they think they can retain everything by memory, and they miss important feedback and action items. Customers appreciate it when they see you taking notes and demonstrating that their feedback is critical for you to capture. At the end of the meeting, you should recap the action items out loud so that both parties are calibrated on what needs to be done.

Ask for the Business (or the Next Step)

Depending on the meeting and where you are in the sales process, you always want to end the meeting with an "ask." That might be asking them if they would like to trial the product or it could be literally asking them for the business if you are in a later stage of the sales process.

Follow Up and Follow Through

Sales is all about following up and following through. You must be very responsive to your customers' needs. Sales is also all about *speed*. You cannot be too busy to call your customer back and help them. They are reaching out to you for a reason and their expectation is that you will get back to them in a timely manner. I am always shocked at how many sales reps do not respond to a customer until days later, or not at all. Help your customers when they ask for help— and always display a high sense of urgency in responding to their needs and wants.

Storming is about putting your sales strategy into action. The preparation, the disciplined selling process, and making the sales call should all work in conjunction with each other so you can position yourself for success. Showing up is important, but you will be more effective when you show up *prepared* and follow a disciplined selling process.

Summary:

- **Preparing for the Sales Call:** Be ready for the sales call.

- **Disciplined Selling Process:** Follow an organized process for managing your sales opportunities.

- **The Sales Call:** Always start with a "thank you!" and end with an "ask."

CHAPTER 5

PRE-PERFORMING – "PREPARE TO WIN"

Everyone in sales knows you have to drive results or you won't have a long career. Sales is all about growth and delivering on other company initiatives. Most sales reps will have a quota that is established every year. This is a sales number that you must hit because companies expect you to deliver on the quota plan. The quota puts a lot of pressure on you, and it is what your compensation is based on.

Pre-Performing is all about setting yourself up for short- and long-term success. I recall a story where I once failed to prepare for a big sales call. It was a large capital equipment opportunity with a large customer. I was a new rep and wasn't aware of how big a deal the opportunity was and thought I could do it alone. I went by myself into the presentation with the customer only to find out that my competitors had teams of three people (the sales rep, the sales manager, and the marketing leader for the product line).

Unfortunately, I did not do a great job selling our product against the competition with their experts who could detail everything about their products. It was a big lesson for me that I needed to make sure I asked for help and I had to be better prepared for a big presentation like this. I remember my customer in the supply chain was an over 30-year veteran, and she told me she was disappointed in my presentation and thought that I could have done much better.

My response to her was filled with pure humility. I admitted I could have done better and that I should have asked for more support. I didn't prepare to perform in that intense environment for a big sale opportunity. It was very unfortunate because we had a great product the customer liked, and I really felt like I let myself, my customer, and my company down.

In a weird twist of fate, I ended up getting the large capital order. My customer said she still liked our product the best and she appreciated the fact I didn't make excuses, didn't pass blame, and took responsibility for being unprepared. It was an unbelievable lesson for me to learn about "selling yourself" and how important it is in life that **when you mess up, you fess up.** We need to own our mistakes and take accountability because most people will forgive you and move on.

Now, we will start to transition into the importance of repeatable consistent results that you need over the course of your career. Pre-Performing is all about learning from our mistakes and working to not make them again. It is also about recognizing what leads to our successful experiences and making sure that we replicate those behaviors to lead to more success. It requires us all to adjust, be willing to change our behaviors/habits, and then adapt to changing conditions because things are constantly evolving. In healthcare, back in the 1980's, most companies would only have one major change initiative in a year; now, you typically see one per quarter. "Selling yourself" and building a career of success requires you to never be satisfied with where you are today because that will never be enough. You should always be looking at ways to continuously improve, especially in sales because you never have all the answers.

PART I: CONTINUOUS IMPROVEMENT MINDSET

"Selling yourself" is a journey of continuous improvement over the course of your professional career. In the Forming chapter, we discussed feedback, coaching, and development as all being part of the Forming process. Continuous improvement is all about never being satisfied with who you are today and always looking for ways to improve. Refining your sales skills will translate into more money in your pocket and will make your job more enjoyable. One way you can continuously improve is with a sales call debrief that a manager can have with you or, alternatively, you can do a self-audit.

Sales Call Debrief

After a sales call, you should always evaluate yourself on what went well and what didn't go well. You own your continuous improvement because nobody will ever care about your professional development as much as you will. You must be honest with yourself about where you need to develop. You can't rely on your original strengths to get you by. The sales call debrief process will help accelerate the learning experience that you will have on the job. We all like to talk about the things we do well; it is much harder to talk about the things we do not do very well. It takes courage to examine yourself, and you need a strong, direct manager who will give you both appreciative and constructive feedback that will make you more effective.

The manager's feedback should be very detailed with examples like, "You should have asked the customer what he disliked about his current vendor." The more direct the feedback is in the sales call debrief, the greater the impact it will have. You don't want a manager just saying you need to ask better probing questions. The sales call debrief is a great opportunity to improve and do better for the next sales call so you can ultimately win! We are all in sales to win and grow the business because that is how we get paid. Every sales rep wants praise and recognition because most sales reps typically like to get positive reinforcement. I think sales reps also pay close attention to their manager's actions and not always their words. The key takeaway is to make sure that you apply the coaching and, hopefully, the managers are living the coaching and feedback they are giving to you as the sales rep.

This process of continuously examining ourselves will help us so much in this Pre-Performing stage. Once we get good at correcting our own performance, we can then start to transition onto things we need to be doing better for our customers. We need to document everything we do for our customers that brings value. I like to call these the sources of value for your customers, and we must always be demonstrating what we are doing to help our customers have a more favorable future.

PART II: SOURCES OF VALUE FOR YOUR CUSTOMERS

The goal is to have a lifetime of success in sales, so it is essential to consistently be bringing value to your customers. Value can come in many different forms so we are going to look at some sources of value that can help you differentiate yourself from your competition. It is important that you document and remind your customers of these sources of value that you are providing to them on a daily, weekly, or monthly basis. Consistent customer delivered value will bring both short- and long-term success.

Professional Guidance

Your goal is to be a top tier sales professional and an expert seller. You will be aiming too low if you just want to be a sales rep. It is important to realize that this is your career, and you should be investing in your skills because you can offer a lot to your customers with your knowledge and experience. You never want to just be considered a glorified customer service rep. The lowest level of a rep is just an order taker, and there is no fun or challenge in this. The goal is to be a trusted subject-matter expert who your customers can count on. The job is so much more fun when you master your craft as the trusted advisor to help your customers.

You can provide professional guidance by being an expert in your product categories. Your customers will appreciate your insights from other customers and hearing about the ways that they are improving by using your products or services. You can provide on-going training and in-services where it makes sense to help the customers know all the important features and benefits of your products. Customers will reward you with their business when they see the professional business acumen that you bring to the job. Once you establish yourself as a professional, it will be important to start to look at the financial impact you can deliver.

Financial Value

Your goal is to bring great financial value to your customer. Most customers want to get great value for what they are buying. There is a saying that goes, **"Price is what you pay, and value is what you get."** The key is to make sure that you don't just sell at the best price because you generally get what you pay for, and many factors go into the price. It is important that you frame your story around the financial offering so the customer truly knows what goes into that price. Customer buying decisions made solely on price can sometimes be bad decisions, so it is the job of the sales rep to really explain the value of the product. The lowest price is not always the best option.

You can provide some great financial tools to highlight the value you are bringing to your customers. It is important to document those financial savings because most customers will have savings goals that they will need to hit so they can get their company bonus payouts. Just make sure you really explain the price and what value the customer is getting with that price. Sometimes customers won't be comparing an equivalent product, unit of measure, or same quality of product. It is important to make sure it is truly an apples-to-apples comparison.

Relationship Value

I have highlighted the relationship value throughout this book. Customer relationships are so important because, when everything else is equal, the customer will buy from the person who they like and trust the most. The job is so much more fun when you make great relationships with your customers– in fact, over time, many will become good friends. We all spend so much time at work that it becomes so much more rewarding when you are doing business with people you genuinely like.

You might consider looking at all your customer contacts by account and ranking them from 1 (hardly knowing them) to 5 (your best customer relationships). In sales, our first objective is to just **"be known"** by customers so they can, at a minimum, connect you to your company and/or your products. Next, you want to advance the relationship over multiple visits to gain likability and your customers will want to do more business with you. Lastly, over time and multiple projects working together, the ultimate goal is to **"be trusted"** because that is the best and most treasured relationship to earn. In summary, a ranking of 1 would be the most basic, lowest level of a customer relationship where you would just be known. A ranking of 3 would be a mid-level relationship where you would be liked but not used primarily. Lastly, a 5 would be the highest level and best relationship with a customer, where you are seen as a trusted advisor. The goal is to be working to move customers from the lowest level of just being known to the highest level of being trusted with every relationship at every account.

Operational Value

Price won't matter to the customer if you can't deliver the product. I like to always call out the operational value because it costs more money to have more inventory, better fill rates, and a better run company to deliver on everything from picking the product to shipping the product. You always want that customer experience to be much more than just the lowest line-item price. In many cases, the company with the lowest-priced product has cut corners in quality with a cheaper product or hasn't made the investment operationally to be able to supply the product. Reps love to sell products that they can count on to ship to the customers. Backorders are challenging because once the product is back in stock, you must start selling it all over again. You should just focus on the products you know your company can deliver on from an operational standpoint so you can bring the most value to your customer.

Political Value

Political value can come in the form of a product or service that can help with safety, a green initiative, or something that the customer is looking for to help their political image. In healthcare, this might be a reusable product that eliminates disposable waste. You want to connect with your customers in ways that will have special meaning to them and the company they work for.

In some cases, you might need to work with someone else who the customer wants you to work with, like another distributor or specialty vendor. Your customer might want you to work with someone else because it is better for them for multiple reasons. It is important to follow your customer's direction and get the political value out of the relationship if it becomes a win for the customer and the other party involved. The key is knowing how you can make it "1 + 1 = 3" to achieve the multiplying factor of working together to attain more.

PART III: SALES TOOLS

I remember once having to make a big sales presentation in Las Vegas to a large contracting organization. My goal was to never again make the mistake I had made when I wasn't prepared to sell the capital product to my customer. This time my plan was to have another teammate there to help me make the sale. I remember thinking to myself, I am going to bring our top rep out of Chicago so that we can position our company as the best option to the panel of customers.

It was like bringing Michael Jordan to a YMCA pick-up game. I remember some of the competitors in the industry seeing us waiting outside in the hallway, and you could literally see fear in their faces. We had brought our products with us, and we were going to show our surgical instruments like fine jewelry as we told our story, with these beautiful instruments laid out against the black velvet product binders that they were in. We always believed in letting the product do the talking because we had the highest quality instruments. We shared the philosophy that because our instruments were of the highest quality in materials and workmanship, you only had to buy them once.

I remember kicking off the meeting with some high-level management selling points about the company, and then I handed off the baton to our top sales professional and let him tell everyone why buying from us was the best option. The story was exceptional, bringing in everything from above, from the sources of value to the professional expertise to the operational value of having the right product at the right time. In addition, the passion and energy he brought was so incredible that the audience was just mesmerized by how much this sales professional loved selling and how proud he was of the products. We were awarded the contract and made some great relationships with customers who were in the room. Because our story was the best story, we won the business. It is important to have the best story prepared for your products and company so that you can consistently have sales success.

You will want to have a strong elevator pitch and a company value proposition to help you tell the story of your company. If you are not provided with these tools, I recommend that you build your own because it's true that **the best story wins when competing for sales opportunities.** You will also want to have a sales playbook to help you with sales messaging.

Elevator Pitch

The elevator pitch is a clear, crisp story of your company or something that you are selling. The elevator pitch can best be described like fishing, which I love to do. First, you need to hook the customers; do this by focusing on their needs in the first 30 seconds. Next, in two minutes or less, you need to start reeling the customer in; focus on the outcomes your product can provide for them. Lastly, in five minutes or less, you need to land them in the boat by closing the sale; provide proof points of why what you are selling is the *best* option.

Outcomes in healthcare generally fall into three main categories: clinical, financial, or operational benefits. You will have an outstanding elevator pitch if your product or service can hit all three of the main outcome categories, and this should result in a guaranteed sale. The goal is to deliver meaningful outcomes towards the needs your customer has. An example would be to have a product or service that can increase revenue and lead to better patient outcomes.

You need proof to make the elevator pitch realistic and attainable. In healthcare, the key is having information and data backed by evidence. This can be in the form of a clinical study conducted by a third-party company or a whitepaper written from the perspective of a doctor who has hands-on experience with your product.

Elevator pitches are very effective and a great way of selling. Every customer appreciates a sales rep who is crystal clear in their offering versus one who is rambling a bunch of unconnected information. You want to learn how to be efficient in your communication delivery and make every word count. This is also nice in your personal life because people appreciate those who speak in facts rather than fluff. If you want to expand your story beyond the elevator pitch, you should start to transition to what we like to call the "company value proposition." This is a longer version of the elevator pitch where you can go much deeper in detail.

Value Proposition

A *value proposition* is a company overview that highlights a set of promises the company can deliver on. You want to have a strong value proposition because it is great to be able to sell the overall picture of the company. Many companies might have many product lines and services that can sometimes be confusing. The value proposition can highlight the best parts of the company and tell the story in a more complete way.

The value proposition will typically highlight your company's history, products, customer service, quality promise, financial value examples, manufacturing and operational values, and any other value-related items. The goal is to demonstrate that the company is vertically integrated with all the business functions that can help support a customer.

The main goal is to show that your company is **"easy to do business with"** because every customer wants to work with companies that make it easy to buy from them. You want to promote your company and all the great products it has to offer, selling yourself in how you will provide wonderful service and support. You want to bring the value proposition's set of promises to reality by following the sales playbook to put into practice all the things you can do for a customer.

Sales Playbook

Another great sales tool offered by many companies is called a sales playbook. It provides company goals, your individual performance goals, your compensation, marketing selling tips, key probing questions, and other valuable information all in one spot. The key is using the information and putting it into practice; you don't want to have your playbook sit on a bookshelf and collect dust. It should be a living, breathing document that you are constantly looking at and updating with best practices and key learnings.

Even professional sports teams have a playbook because they know how important it is that everyone is on the same page with what it takes to win. **You want to work hard to not just get it right, but to not ever get it wrong.** The sales playbook was very helpful when I was a rep. It gave me the right focus and perspective on how everything fits together. It helps keep you laser-focused on the key priorities.

If you are in sales at a company that doesn't prepare a sales playbook for you, you should consider building your own. Take all the great information you get from training classes and feedback from managers and put it all in one place. I created my own sales playbook because I was always focused on making things easier for myself to help me be more effective in selling myself.

Sales Pipeline

A sales pipeline is a visual representation of sales opportunities and where they are in the purchasing process (e.g. the stages I described in the last chapter—target, active, commit). These stages represent the opportunities at the various points in the sales process, from initial demand generation to the service/support stage we discussed in the Storming chapter.

Why is the Sales Pipeline the most important tool?

The sales pipeline is a reflection of your sales process activities. It keeps you laser-focused on prioritizing what is most important so that you can be efficient and effective. It becomes the "lifeblood of the company" because, if you have multiple reps, it will combine everyone's opportunities into these stages. It is the source of truth for sales people, and managers will ask questions from it to hold you accountable to delivering on your sales results.

In the last chapter of the book, we will highlight the best practices around the sales pipeline. The best reps work hard with lots of sales activity that leads to many sales opportunities that then leads to a robust sales pipeline. **Sales Process Activity + Sales Pipeline = Sales Results**

Summary:

- **Continuous Improvement Mindset:** Have a mindset to always get better.

- **Sources of Value for Your Customers:** Deliver and document value to your customer.

- **Sales Tools:** Employ sales tools to help you win.

CHAPTER 6

PERFORMING – "WIN THE DAY"

The sales professional I talked about in my "Best Story Wins" story is the best example I have seen of *Performing*. He is the best sales rep I have ever worked with, and he consistently performed, making his quota 38 out of 42 years. This history of strong performance is unheard of in any healthcare device sales company and really is incredible in any industry, any company, or any sales job. He had three different geographic territories that he covered in his career and was successful in all of them. It proves many reps wrong who say, "if I only had that person's territory, I would be successful." Let's look at *why* he was so successful and how you can implement some of his strategies to consistently sell yourself.

This person had relationships that were deep and wide in every one of his accounts. He took great pride in knowing lots of people in different departments and **everyone was important to him.** His customer relationships meant the world to him and many of his customers became good friends of his. His work ethic was second to none, and he wouldn't mind driving late on a Friday afternoon to deliver a product to his customer because it was the right thing to do.

He also said he **made decisions with the long-term goal in mind.** He never wanted to make a short-term decision that would negatively impact his relationships. Sales was always about a career to him and not just a job. He wore a tie and sports coat every day because he wanted to stand out and always look professional. His knowledge and experience were unmatched, and he combined this with a burning desire to win, making him an unstoppable force. He is first class and has high integrity in everything he does, refusing to accept mediocrity in anything.

So, *how do you consistently hit your numbers every year and perform at the highest level in sales?* It is really a combination of everything I have shared as building blocks to success. Additionally, the best companies will have a great process around goals, scoreboards, and performance management to help drive accountability. We will get to the quantitative results, but we will first examine the qualitative results being "the how" of driving results.

PART I: QUALITATIVE RESULTS – "THE HOW"

"Getting results the right way" is a common saying you will hear in sales. The key with getting sales *the right way* is the qualitative aspect of selling. You won't have a very long career in sales if nobody likes you– even if you are getting short-term results. When you consider that the most important aspect in sales is the relationships, then it is critical that you really do business the right way by always putting your customer first. You want to operate in sales with some core values (which are sometimes called core competencies) that set the standard for how you conduct business from a qualitative standpoint in sales.

Core Values

Integrity

Integrity is the first main core value because it is the foundation of everything. You want to operate with integrity in everything that you do. To me, **integrity is making sure our words and actions are aligned.** In sales, you can't overpromise and underdeliver because that is a major integrity hit. You want to treat everyone the way they want to be treated and to be honest in how you conduct business. It always bothers me when people say, "Can I be honest with you?" You want to *always* be honest in everything you do, so you shouldn't have to qualify a statement by asking that. Work hard to make sure you stand by your word and always do the right thing for your customers.

Customer-Focused

Customer-focused is a core value you must have since we have talked at length about the importance of relationships. The customers' needs and wants drive everything we do in sales. It is important to have a "customer-first mentality" in every decision that you make. Being customer-focused sets your mindset to automatically put the needs of your customers ahead of everything else.

Energy

Energy is another key core value that is totally in your control. You want to be that person who brings energy to everything you do because **people love being around people who are great creators of energy.** You want to build collective energy with your teammates and company so you can generate great value for your customers. Also, you want to bring great energy to your customers so they see how excited you are to engage with them.

Active Listening

Active listening is important so that you truly understand your customers' needs. **The best reps**

are great listeners. The misconception about most great sales people is that everyone thinks that they are great talkers. Sales is more about listening than talking. Customers will give you all the information you need to be able to sell them products. Take great pride in being an active listener so that you can be an exceptional sales representative. Truly *listen* to your customers without interrupting them by blurting out what you want to say. Let the customer finish their thoughts because their words are filled with priceless information that will ultimately help you to sell better.

These core values will help to mold you into a successful sales professional. Next, I want to focus on some examples of sales principles that will make these core values more actionable and visible. You can write these yourself. I made these into "I will" statements that force you to operate with a very dedicated mindset.

PART II: SALES PRINCIPLES

I think it is important to have sales principles that drive you to sustained excellence. These principles will keep you laser-focused on the quantitative and qualitative results. They all start with "I will" as "I will" statements will lead you to commit to these principles.

Principle I: I will consistently meet or exceed sales quota and performance goals/ tactics for the company.

This reinforces that everything is about driving results. It is the first principle because you need a growth mindset in *everything* that you do.

Principle II: I will live the company mission, vision, and values.

It is important that you live the mission, vision, and values because this is the manner in which the company expects you to conduct business.

Principle III: I will hold myself to a higher standard in everything that I do.

You should always strive to be world class.

Principle IV: I will sell with honesty and integrity, focusing on the long-term sale.

This principle is all about the long-term horizon and never making bad short-term decisions that could potentially take advantage of the customer. You don't want to just get the one order; the goal is to get all future orders over many years.

Principle V: I will be a great team player.

This principle is all about the team! I believe that in sales it takes a total team effort from a sales rep getting the order, to customer service taking the order, to someone picking/packing/shipping the order to the customer.

Principle VI: I will always put my customers first.

You want to have a customer-first mentality in everything that you do.

Principle VII: I will always strive to out-work, out-want, and out-sell my competition.

This principle is all about being a grinder. Just go get the business and want the business more than anyone else.

These principles will help you to elevate your performance in how you do the job. The next part is to know the quantitative objectives you are expected to hit.

PART III: QUANTITATIVE RESULTS – "THE WHAT"

The qualitative results are "the how" and are very important with respect to the way in which you will conduct business. **You will still always need to deliver quantitative results in sales.** The quantitative sales results are "the what" and it is essential that you achieve these. You will have metrics for these sales results that you will be measured against. Some of these key metrics are highlighted below.

Sales Quota

Every sales rep is assigned an annual quota with the sales number they need to hit for the year. The quota is based on the prior year's sales plus additional growth dollars based on the growth expectations of the company. If you are working for a new company, the quota will be based on the budget growth dollars that management is expected to achieve.

Sales is like being on a performance treadmill because you are always being evaluated against metrics that measure how much you have sold, which products you have sold, what price you sold the products at, and how you sold them. The key is staying laser-focused on the metrics and being disciplined to work hard every day to deliver on the quota. The story of the sales rep making his quota 38 out of 42 years is so remarkable because of the external factors that can impact quota, like a bad economy, lack of funding, customer changes, and internal issues with your own company like backorders, no new products, etc. **Your goal is to make your sales quota every year.** You will also have some other quantitative goals besides quota if you work for a well-run company. The payoff for making your sales quota is that your manager won't be questioning you or your sales results when you are hitting your sales numbers!

Sales Goals (MBO's or Performance Goals)

In addition to an assigned quota with growth dollars, you will typically be given goals that relate to actions the company wants you to take to hit the number. Some companies will call them MBO's or Management Business Objectives. An example of a qualitative MBO would be an objective of using a CRM tool like Salesforce daily to store your customer targeting. At other times, there are quantitative goals. Some examples would be needing to have three new opportunities a week and one win per week and spending 30 minutes a day putting the sales information into Salesforce. You could have quotas on certain product lines as well, or even a quota on a new product launch that can be captured in your other sales goals.

Summary:

- **Qualitative Results – "The How":** Be dedicated to getting results the right way.

- **Sales Principles:** Create "I will" statements to stay focused.

- **Quantitative Results – "The What":** Focus on hitting your quota and achieving your other sales goals.

CHAPTER 7

OVERACHIEVING – "RISE TO THE NEXT LEVEL"

Be exceptional. Overachieving is all about doing everything well from Pre-Forming to Performing. It is a mindset that you want to be the best of the best.

The last chapter was all about performance and making your sales numbers. Now, we take it up a notch to the level of overachieving. We are going to look at the best traits of overachievers, the best processes they follow, and the best ways they organize their work.

PART I: BEST PEOPLE

In addition to The Foundational Four of Personal Drive, Winning Attitude, People Skills, and Results-Driven, the most successful sales reps I've seen have these characteristics that make them the best of the best:

Being a Grinder

Having a relentlessly strong work ethic. Committed to out-working everyone and being the hardest working person in the room.

Making the Extra Effort

Going the extra mile in everything they do. Never settling for mediocrity or the status quo in anything. Strong belief that the extra effort will yield more results.

Competitive

Wanting to compete and win at everything.

Self-Disciplined

Consistently practicing good habits.

Skilled Negotiator

Negotiating effectively with all people, especially customers.

Relationship Builder

Building quality, long-lasting relationships.

Loves Commission-Based Jobs

Wanting more variable pay with higher upside than a fixed salary.

Change Agent

Willing to adapt and embrace changing conditions.

Dedicated

Committed to taking the time in the territory to build relationships and become a product expert.

PART II: BEST PROCESS

A great process is important to overachieving. In sales, the process is having consistent sales activity that leads to a strong sales pipeline.

Sales Activity (Customer Interactions)

Sales activity is all about steady forward movement doing activities that will lead to increased sales. Overachievers are really effective at selling in all modalities.

Face-to-Face Visits

Top performers prefer face-to-face visits because they can see opportunities besides just relying on questions. For example, you might be meeting with a customer who has a project highlighted on a whiteboard that could be a potential opportunity for you.

Phone

Elite sellers find a way to make the most of their time using the phone to call customers in between face-to-face visits.

Text Messages

Top reps will contact customers on their cell phones with text messages to give quick updates or ask a question.

Email

The highest performers know how to write emails that are crisp, clear, and to the point.

The opportunities generated from these customer interactions lead to the second part of the process: populating the sales pipeline.

Sales Pipeline

The best reps' sales pipelines have some key qualities, as detailed below.

Quantity

They have plenty of sales opportunities to hit their yearly sales quota. Most experts say you need your total sales opportunity dollars to be three to five times your growth dollars (the "new dollars" portion of your sales quota that is in addition to the reoccurring base business in your territory). Because you will not win every opportunity you target, it is important that your opportunities' dollar total is much higher than your overall sales quota.

Quality

They have qualified opportunities that have a champion and a good probability of closing.

Balance

They have a strong balance of small, medium, and large opportunities along with balanced representation of the products (if the portfolio is diversified).

Velocity

They have opportunities that move quickly through the sales pipeline from target to commit.

The sales pipeline is really the source of truth based on your activity that reflects all your opportunities in one place, allowing you to track how you plan to hit your quota.

PART III: BEST APPROACH

The last key element to overachieving is your organization around all the information you gain which will lead to **"Ruthless Prioritization"** of where and how you will spend your time to hit your number. You will need to utilize the right tools to help you make consistent progress towards your goals.

Folders

You should keep folders for your current projects and key priorities for your customers. You want to be very disciplined and organized with the customer information you obtain from sales calls. By referencing this information, you can start each customer conversation where you left off at the end of the last discussion. This shows respect and professionalism to your customer and makes your meetings more efficient and effective.

Notebook/CRM

Keep all important meeting notes in a spiral notebook. The spiral notebook allows you to take notes in real-time and capture the customer feedback. It also helps you to display that you are actively listening. After your sales calls or at the end of the day in your home office, you should make updates in your company's CRM. The electronic CRM becomes your living database of customer information that is current and accurate. The CRM should hold customer contact information, opportunities, sales reporting, and any other key notes pertaining to the customers.

To-Do Lists

The ultimate organizational tool is your hot list of sales priorities. You will want to practice what I like to call "Ruthless Prioritization" to force rank your to-do list. During this exercise, you will place your most urgent and important priorities at the top of your list and put the less important ones at the bottom. Top reps have a list of to-do's for every day and every week to be successful. One rep I knew had what he called the "grocery list" on the back of an envelope; this was his to-do list of actions he had to execute on at the end of the year so he could hit his sales number.

Overachieving is the result of putting it all together! You must have the right characteristics of an overachiever because it starts with a mindset of wanting to be excellent in everything you do. A great sales process ensures that you advance your sales opportunities through the stages of your sales pipeline. Lastly, the organization around the important priorities will help you make the best use of your time and effort!

Summary:

- **Best People:** Embody the key characteristics of overachievers.

- **Best Process:** Be disciplined in following a great process.

- **Best Approach:** Practice "Ruthless Prioritization" to do what is urgent and important first.

CLARITY, CONFIDENCE, AND COMMITMENT

I would like to conclude with the three C's of clarity, confidence, and commitment. One of my first mentors would say a mantra they had at their company: **"Clarity creates confidence, and confidence creates commitment."**

Clarity

Now that you've read this book, you should have a much better idea of what it takes to be successful in sales. You can start to build your career in sales or, if you are already in sales, you can go to the next level. If you start early enough, you'll have the chance to work hard and get promoted multiple times in your career. I was fortunate enough to earn some promotions, and my hope is that you will get promoted faster and more often.

My plan was to provide you with the roadmap of how you can be successful and sell yourself. Many books focus on only one aspect of "selling yourself" and my book was designed to look at the entire process. The plan was to keep it simple and consolidated because I didn't want it to be complicated. I hope you have a clear picture of what it takes to have a successful career in sales.

Confidence

After reading this book, you should have more confidence in "selling yourself." So much of sales is having confidence because you must be fearless without any self-doubt. I want everyone to be more confident and execute in the ways they can be better instead of always thinking why they cannot do something.

My confidence really took off when the same person who told me to knock on the CEO's door said that there are not any doors you can't open in life. He told me he thought I could be a CEO someday if I worked hard enough and did everything I could to get the right knowledge, have hands-on experience, and deliver winning results. There is nothing more powerful than someone believing in you and telling you that you can be anything you want to be in life. I encourage you all to build your confidence by finding mentors. Great sales results and strong customer relationships will help you gain confidence. Further, your confidence will grow with time in your territory and experience on the job.

Commitment

Being successful in your sales career takes a lot of commitment. You cannot just have talent because a lot of talented people will never be successful. You also can't just work hard because you must have the right skills to put it all together. The commitment is so critical to working hard and using the talents you have because most of us do not have all the cards in the deck. You can still be wildly successful if you are dedicated to doing the requirements of your job..

Work can be fun and should be fun! The most successful teams I have worked on weren't always the most talented but they were always the most committed. Winners just find a way to win. In most cases, everyone knows what must be done, but many people aren't willing to do what it takes to be successful. Commitment is so important in all aspects of life because most things worth achieving do not come very easily.

Remember, the most important aspect of a sales call will always be about "selling yourself." The world is filled with mediocrity . . . don't let yourself become a member of the "cult of the average." "Selling yourself" always starts with *believing* in yourself.

You have no limits to what you can accomplish in life! You now have the clarity of what needs to be done to sell yourself, you should have the confidence to do what is required to sell yourself, and finally the commitment just comes down to doing it.

ABOUT THE AUTHOR

Bryan Fosmore serves as Vice President of U.S. Sales and is responsible for all U.S.-based commercial sales at IZI Medical. He is a sales executive with over 25 years of experience in the medical device industry. Prior to IZI Medical, Bryan served as Senior Vice President of U.S. Commercial Sales at Symmetry Surgical, Senior Vice President of Sales at Aspen Surgical and National Vice President of Sales for V. Mueller. Bryan is a proven sales executive who has driven growth by developing and managing complex channels, markets, products, and customer initiatives. Bryan earned his B.A. in Marketing from Alma College.

BEST ADVICE IN SALES

I wanted to end the book with some of the best advice I've received from mentors that I didn't use in the book chapters. I hope this advice can help you "Sell Yourself!"

- **Professional Best Folder** - You should have what I call a "Professional Best Folder." This is where I keep important information I have learned from mentors, training, and industry meetings. I refer to this folder all the time to get inspiration or ideas of ways to look at things differently in sales.

- **Personal Best Folder** - You should also have a "Personal Best Folder." This is where I keep motivational quotes and key thoughts from leaders outside my professional network. This is very helpful to look at and read because it keeps you grounded and gives you perspective.

- **Go where it is hot** - You should go visit customers who have lots going on with projects and are spending lots of money.

- **Be brief, be brilliant, be gone** - You should always be crisp and clear in your sales messaging.

- **Half a donut time selling to an executive** - You should make your sales points in the time it takes to eat half a donut.

- **Have ant-like discipline** - You should do the repeatable activities over and over and over again . . . It takes ant-like discipline doing the boring and mundane things better than anyone else.

- **Do it right the first time** - You should never cut corners.

- **Have a high sense of urgency in all you do** - You should always operate with a fast pace.

- **People listen to what you do vs. what you say** - You should always have a bias for action.

- **More doing and less talking** - You should be a doer.

- **Big hat and no cattle** - You should never be seen as a talker and not a doer.

- **Healthy tension** - You should never be afraid to put some pressure on a customer to make a decision.

- **Get up on the balcony to look at the dance floor** - You should always look at the overall picture.

- **We will get there** - You should believe you and your team can always get to the finish line.

- **Little hinges open big doors** - You should remember that the little things matter.

- **Quality time left** - You should make every day count.

- **Do more than is expected** - You should never just do the minimum requirements.

- **You never outperform your inner circle** - You should always surround yourself with great people.

- **Work like it is a privilege** - You should be grateful that you have a job in sales.

- **If you are going to do something, do it with a smile on your face** - You should take positive energy into everything you do and show it with your body language.

If you can "sell yourself," you will be able to sell anything in life!

You are ready to sell yourself!

There is an ocean of opportunities waiting for you.

Good Luck!

Good Selling!

Go "Sell Yourself!"

Made in the USA
Monee, IL
13 December 2022

21688700R00069